THE
WALKING
- AWAY
WORLD

KENNETH
PATCHEN

BOOKS BY KENNETH PATCHEN
AVAILABLE FROM NEW DIRECTIONS

Collected Poems

In Quest of Candlelighters

The Journal of Albion Moonlight

Memoirs of a Shy Pornographer

Selected Poems

Sleepers Awake

The Walking-Away World

   Wonderings

   Hallelujah Anyway

   But Even So

We Meet

   Because It Is

   Poemscapes

   A Letter To God

   Hurrah For Anything

   Aflame and Afun of Walking Faces

KENNETH PATCHEN

The Walking-Away World

Introduction by Jim Woodring

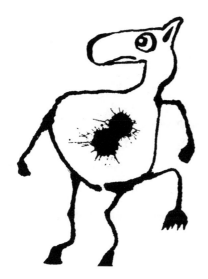

 A NEW DIRECTIONS BOOK

Publishers Note: *The Walking-Away World* collects three New Directions Kenneth Patchen titles: *Hal-lelujah Anyway* (1960), *But Even So* (1968), and *Wonderings* (1971), previously available only in separate editions.

Manufactured in the United States of America
Cover and front matter by Rodrigo Corral Design/Christopher Brand
Interior composition by Arlene Goldberg
New Directions Books are printed on acid-free paper.
First published as New Directions Paperbook 1114 in 2008

Library of Congress Cataloging-in-Publication Data

Patchen, Kenneth, 1911–1972.
  The Walking-away world / Kenneth Patchen ; introduction by Jim Woodring.
    p. cm.—(New directions paperbook ; 1116)
  ISBN 978-0-8112-1757-6 (pbk. : acid-free paper)
  I. Title.
  PS3531.A764A6 2008b
  811'.54—dc22   2008019586

New Directions Books are published for James Laughlin
by New Directions Publishing Corporation
80 Eighth Avenue, New York, NY 10011

CONTENTS

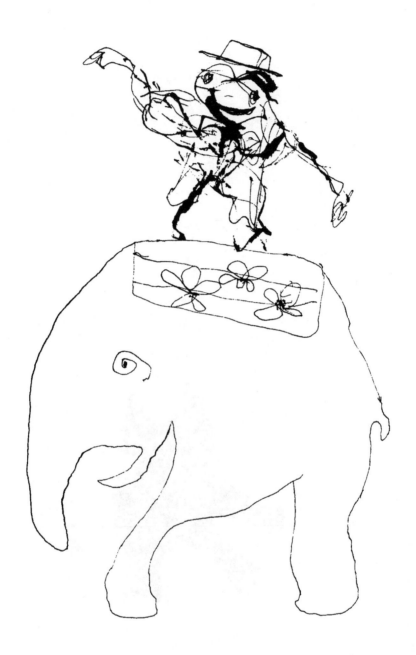

LOOKING AT KENNETH PATCHEN

by Jim Woodring

Once, in a moment of weakness, I bought a book that was intended to teach artists with no business savvy how to market and sell their work. I settled down to read it and got as far as halfway through the introduction, where it said:

"Many people believe that artists are special beings with special powers, who perform some sort of mystical service for the world that only they can provide. Nothing could be further from the truth! Artists are ordinary people like everyone else. They have their job to do, just as the plumber has his. The plumber fixes pipes; the artist creates art."

It says a lot about the greatness of America that a person can write and publish such dangerous, inflammatory rubbish here without going to jail. God only knows how many fresh young sapheads that book steered away from secure and socially sanctioned careers and into the uncharted realms of obsession where artists do their dreadful night wrestling.

Yes, of course I know that at the most fundamental level everyone is divine which is to say *ordinary*. But was there ever a wild and yearning youth who saw the words *YOU WILL BE A PLUMBER* written in the sky in letters of flame? Was there ever a plumber who plied his or her trade as a compulsive vocation, mad for pipes, desperate to install them even where they were not wanted, making almost no money and enduring the harshest critical attacks for their efforts decade after decade until they tumbled, still brazing, into their grave? Well, perhaps there was. If so, that plumber was an artist, and is to be pitied.

To state the obvious, artists *are* extraordinary people because of their willingness to take a lifetime of poundings in order to externalize their vision and create the myths of the world that guide, inform, and exalt the rest of mankind. It's one of the things we love about them. There is something pathologically compelling in the biography of a man or woman who willingly submits to the tortures of the damned in order to find the perfect shade of pink to put with greenish grey, or the perfect little phrase of melody, or the perfect three words to express God.

Which brings us to Kenneth Patchen. His reward for doggedly devoting himself to the exploration of the loftiest themes available to a creator and for inventing many new forms through which to express them was poverty and ridicule. Sure, he had fans and supporters, and there were several periods when he had reason to hope that he would achieve the recognition he craved and, many would say, deserved.

But the big payoff never came and the meager recognition he attained wasn't adequate to compensate for the critical drubbings his works usually received. It wasn't nearly enough for a man who kept pulling God down from the sky and into the bookstores.

He responded once to all the negative criticism with an act of almost masochistic toughness; on the inside dust jacket of his book *Cloth of the Tempest* he compiled not a collection of laudatory blurbs but some of the most egregious attacks on his work. Under the heading "WHAT SOME CRITICS HAVE SAID OF PATCHEN'S POETRY:" we read:

"The biggest collection of arrant nonsense ever printed in America"
                                        —*The Springfield (Mass.) Republican*

"Patchen is not a serious poet. And his fulsome self-indulgence, combined with the continual intrusion of a personality that insists on talking, singing, weeping, fighting, and cooing to itself, is very trying . . . "
                                                            —*The Nation*

There are 10 more. Needless to say they had the effect of making his fans feel even more devoted to their talking, singing, weeping, fighting and cooing hero.

He never lost the adolescent's outrage at the cruelty and stupidity of men, and thereby acquired the unwanted reputation as a poet that appealed mostly to young people, a poet to be outgrown after the unreasoning storms of youth had blown over. (I must admit my own appreciation for his work followed exactly that trajectory. I read a great deal of it when I was in my teens and early 20's and by the time I was 30 I regarded my previous veneration of him with embarrassment. That's the cruelty and stupidity of men for you. Nevertheless, I kept copies of his books and revisited them over the years, so when I finally got over my idiotic disdain for heartfelt simplicity I was able to appreciate more than before the rarity and value of his genius, altruism and bravery.)

Kenneth Patchen was always an experimenter and innovator. He pioneered concrete poetry a decade before the concept had its name in his 1946 masterpiece *Sleepers Awake,* the talismanic doorstop that sustained me throughout high school. In that book he bent and distorted the rules of typography to the extent that at a certain point words disappear entirely and are replaced by frantic and explosive designs, as if the book itself were suffering a breakdown under the weight of the horrors contained in it.

With his transcendent love of God and his rough treatment on Earth it's not surprising that Patchen experienced life as a union of joy and despair, as exemplified by the aching title *Hallelujah Anyway.* Like the Christians he saw light in divinity and darkness in man; unlike them he could take no comfort in a promise of Heaven. Like the Vedantists, he saw God everywhere; unlike them he could not forgive men their evildoing. In short, there was no way out for him. Perhaps he would have been happier if he had been able to inhabit a middle zone, the sweet-and-sour gray world most men live in. But he couldn't. He lived in the willful awareness of a tantalizing bliss even as he dwelt in agony.

By "agony" I mean not just the moral torment that such a supersensitive person experiences at the contemplation of life's endless cruelties, but the physical sort.

Patchen spent most of his adult life in pain thanks to a back injury he sustained in 1937 while helping a friend with his car. He was just 26 at the time. He suffered almost constantly until an operation alleviated most of the problem in 1950. Another operation in 1956 restored his health sufficiently that he was able to tour and perform poetry readings with jazz accompaniments.

This idyll lasted only until 1959, when he went into the hospital for another surgery, intended to complete the cure. The word "botched" always occurs in accounts of this episode; one version is that he somehow fell off the operating table. In any event, something happened that permanently and irreparably damaged his spine and plunged him into a debilitating torment that lasted for the thirteen years he had left to him.

The picture-poems (as they are officially known) in this collection were created during those last thirteen years. Under these circumstances it was perhaps impossible for him to write with the sustained effort of will that enabled him to compose the long-form poetry and experimental novels of his earlier years. The picture-poems in their brevity and compactness became a logical mode of expression for a pain-wracked man who could neither get out of bed nor be comfortable lying in it.

And yet this approach was not a compromise. He had made paintings utilizing words throughout his career and regarded them as an intrinsic part of his oeuvre. "It happens that very often my writing with pen is interrupted by my writing with brush, but I think of both as writing," he once told an interviewer. "In other words, I don't consider myself a painter. I think of myself as someone who has used the medium of painting in an attempt to extend."

He certainly did that. The picture-poems have no known antecedents in Western art. Their closest known relatives are the engravings of William Blake, which are not really very much like them. Blake made his words part of his overall compositions, but the two elements remain separate; they are drawings with words. In the picture poems Patchen draws the words as part of the image; they are drawings *of* words, and the way they are drawn determines the way they affect our minds. He can make his phrases flow like trickles of mercury or stick like a bone in the throat. He makes us hear them the way he wants us to hear them.

It may come as a surprise to learn that most of the picture-poems were created in color. In this as well as everything else he did, Patchen was an original. He used every medium he could lay his hands on: dip pen, felt pen, pencil, ink, watercolor, tempera, casein, acrylic, collage and God only knows what else. In a way they look clumsy and naive, like children's drawings, but they have an intuitive mastery of composition and color that could never have been learned in art school. He used color passionately, and it made the words in his pictures scream, mourn and exalt. They glow like portentous neon signs in a dream, like incantations burning in a shaman's brain, like the writing on the wall.

To say that Patchen was not a natural draughtsman is an understatement. He was not a draughtsman at all. There is nothing in any of his pictures that indicate that he could have drawn anything from life. There are no human faces that are more than simple daubs.

What he did have was that most vital quality in the visual artist's tool kit: authority. Did he aspire to draw better? There is no reason to believe it. His pictures did not evolve over the decades. What he drew, he drew, and there it was, solid and real. Is it enough? It is everything.

Much has been written about the creatures that inhabit these works. They are usually described as whimsical, cheerful, friendly-seeming little sprites from some enchanted forest wanting to make friends and play with us. People generally think they are cute as the dickens.

They seem like that to me too . . . until I look at them for a few seconds too long. Then they change into frightening little beasts from the realm of the unspeakable that make the monsters of Hieronymus Bosch look silly and contrived. The staring eyes which were so innocent and endearing a few moments before suddenly seem to me to exude real madness and pain. The ones without mouths stop reminding me of Hello Kitty and starts making me think of H.P. Lovecraft. (Is it just me or does anyone else feel that way about them? Well, it doesn't matter. These are *my* Patchen beasts, dear to my scared little heart, and I wouldn't have them any other way.)

About his words very little can be said. They are so stripped-down and direct that they can only be either accepted or rejected. I can't imagine an editor telling Patchen how to tighten up or improve his writing any more than I can imagine a zookeeper making suggestions on how to improve the design of the tiger.

My favorites among the hundreds of picture-poems I've seen are the ones with just a sentence or two; the ones of twenty words or less, so to speak. For one thing the words are bigger, louder and better formed. For another the designs are usually simpler and more powerful. Consider these examples from *Hallelujah Anyway*:

"Snow is the only one of us that leaves no tracks"

"I PROCLAIM THIS INTERNATIONAL SHUT YOUR BIG
FLAPPING MOUTH WEEK"

"IN THE LONG RUN This is a race where everybody ends up in a tie, sorta"

And these from *But Even So*:

"QUIET WE MUST NOT DISTURB THE EVENING-BEING DEVICE"

"Caring is the only daring Oh you know it"

Patchen was a master of hard-hitting brevity. He frequently gives you more food for thought in a short piece than in a longer one. His best one-liners are as good as his poem and book titles, which I think are among his greatest poetic achievements. It is always exhilarating to read the list of his book titles, which seem to be chapter headings from the Book of Life.

Consider the title of one of his weakest books, a mundane love novel which New Directions founder James Laughlin said Patchen wrote in a desperate attempt to appeal to a wider audience:

See You in the Morning

It was a phrase I used to use without thinking until Patchen shone the light of his selective genius on it and allowed me to see it for what it is: an excruciatingly tender, pathetic expression of hope. Millions upon millions of us utter that exact phrase every night; why do we not then weep, melt, fall into our loved one's arms and cover them in tearful kisses, knowing that the morning when we will *not* see them is coming sooner than we think? If Patchen has his way, we will.

Patchen's work is not to be approached lightly. To take one of his books off the shelf and look into it is to open yourself to an intense emotional experience that can really get to you and change your mood for the rest of the day. He can make you feel terribly sad for yourself, and all your sisters and brothers, known and unknown, living and dead, who have experienced this terrifying and beautiful place. But even so he can also charge you up with enthusiasm for life's fantastic opportunities and make you determined to do what you can for the world.

Buried in the tumbling avalanche of *Sleepers Awake* are a few lines that sum up what Kenneth Patchen's work says to me:

A bit of green grass—a bird—hell it only takes a little to give us all there is anyway.

WONDERINGS

for Miriam

But if your precious
illusion should turn out
not to be real   where then
will you leap, my little flea

Any who live stand alone in one place together

And it is true, it is true
I saw the ships
beautiful as ever
maiden singing

in a dream

Yes,

I saw the ships   but
they were all sailing
away

To Whomever
These village fires
Still have meaning

O may your own most secret
& most beautiful Animal of Light
Come safely to you

The Great Fly Fleet

Steaming into the Sunset
The tossing hair of the Sea-Fellow
Turning the color of scarlet sugar
Under their sticky little keels
"Oh Captain! Hey there, Captain dear...
The Big Wet One, again he threatens to scratch."
"So-oo? Up with them anchors then, you dopes!
— Besides, how many times must I tell you?!
We've got to get out of this world!"

11

O honor the bird
That opened the word
That found the world
That Love might live

O choose the wonder
That knelt on the water
That sun & wind made move
And Love O it shall flame
Though darkness quell
Each and every name

ALLLIGHT SAVING TIME

Turn your clocks
sideways
to the hour
where
no- body
can get a good clean
shot at you

Binding the quiet into chalky sheaves
I do not forget to pack spirit-moss
And lonely isles of "hasty leaves"
Into these "boxes" which will toss
Upon the sea until next Wednesday
When some good soul knowing them mine
Shall bring them back without a word—
And inside I'll find sixteen baby foxes
Sleeping at the breast of a great milk-white bird

18

IN BACK OF

EVERY REALLY THOUGHTFUL CHICKEN

Is some motherly egg or other
Smiling chalkily (although bald)
~Until it gets popped into a pan

Or mauled by a train or marauding elk
But from the leg of that hickory tree
A dappled little pelican beams down on me

Believe that apples could talk

if they had a mind too

WHAT INDEED!

If I am Higgs and he is Humberson
If I am that rich and he's without a cent
Then why can't I at least go down
To my Aunt Lettie's on the seashore
And use one of the spare rooms
Perhaps the one with the disappearing floor
Until, say, Delia or Joan can get there,
Or until some chance winder bops up?
What's the good of being Higgs otherwise

23

With one tiny stick

To arrange the air over the eating-shed

And the evil part of the earth around it

So that at last

Not even the stick is left

24

25

O "listen" is like an elephant
Who stalks the woods at night
& with his mole-soft & curling trunk
Touches all the stars with light
& written on his nobly gentle sides
Are the names of trees & fields & men
Of where we shall go tomorrow
And of what it will be like then

KEEP IT

Keep it in the hither
It will gleam
Keep it from their weather
It's your ice cream
Hide it in the queen's room
O don't you be mean
Hide it in that cleanest kingdom
Where it won't ever be seen
'Cause, brother, that's your only ice cream

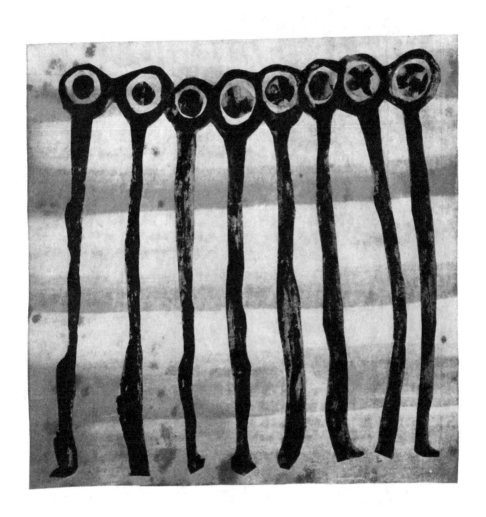

The Broom Of Bells

Has swept a path for her

From village windows
The voices of children
Fill her name with cool flowers

Thus at sweet evening

Welcome we this lovely one

30

Since in the
patient eye
of mouse & swan & fly
all our plagues
& conflagrations glide
as dust upon
the uncaring wind

33

If You Can Lose Your Head

When all aground you
Are busy clothing bares
Then we may let you in
To greet a rather different kind of King

This is "the Animal That Walks Sitting Down"
It is not an animal you can tire easily
In addition I am looking up at the sky
And if a voice suddenly shouts down out of that cloud
I'm sure it will most certainly say
Good luck everybody!

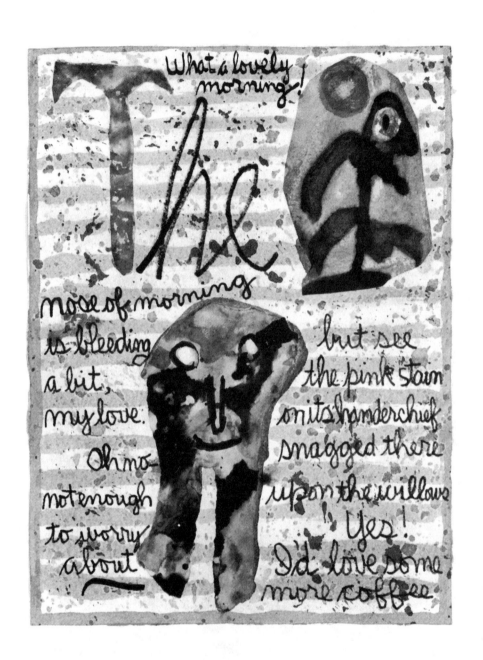

What a lovely morning!

The nose of morning is bleeding a bit, my love.

Oh no— not enough to worry about ——

but see the pink stain on its handerchief snagged there upon the willows. Yes! I'd love some more coffee

The Moment

Before the girl picking field daisies

Becomes the girl picking field daisies

There is a moment of some complexity

I see again that Giraffe-of-Sofas
Who at morning leaves snippets of old films
In his grateful and explosive wake
Here are fishes with smiling human faces

Canoeing along banks lined with green-backed bushes
Here are questioning little fellows (λ λ λ λ)
Riding upside down in stiff-collar wagons

Here from a rainbarrel the limp ear of Wednesday
Dangles beside a porcupine bouquet

41

Let us rejoice, then, remembering all the grand (but deserved) things that some-how never managed to come our way

HOUSE ON HORSEBACK

The drover follows along
Not to earn
the opal-encrusted
whistle
promised him

But only to be within an ace of coming through
What he hasn't the least idea of
It's just that it has
such a pretty lilt to it

43

GARRITY
THE GAMBLING
MAN
... GROWN OLD

Once Memphis Grandee of the Quick-Chill Deck
Now at rainy 3 a.m. out of Dallas T
And all the pretty queens have long since gone hagging
All the brave jack-o-knights have been shunted down slack's lane
O Garrity - once the best of all the river's best -
This is what it comes to then
A sick old man in a smelly daycoach
Riding nowhere through the night
Without a lousy dime to his name

TO "RUN THE CROWN

You go down a little below all pride
Where, on the bursting, emerald air
Salamanders ride & pretty periwinkles hide
On the bent steps of Moon Inn
All considerably begun that's modestly done
So only moving in seashell & turtle's sleep
You soon lie down on a sinless bed
And understand what understanding never meant
And why the Bride of Mountains may not weep

O quietly the SUN-MAN sits
In his chair above the world.
Here the old men are blundering liars,
And the young men are cheated of life;
But the golden hands caress all alike.
    O a hundred thousand no ones
        Proclaiming life a fraud —
    A hundred hundred thousand no ones
With just themselves to blame, not God.

50

The words that speak up
from the mangled bodies
of human beings

This
is
the
fallout

that covers everything

on
earth
now

52

QUICK THINKER

Someone has left a wave
In front of the barn?
It grabs hold of the cow.
Poor Grandma has to dismount.

Her skirt gets caught.
The sky catches on fire,
The wave goes to work
And soon puts it out.
Someone sure used his bean!

The monument-maker is little fellow

He could use a hot supper

Instead he goes in he asks the real estate man

"What you got about this size

With a great big forest here

And maybe a great huge big forest right there"

(About the size of fifty Pennsylvanias!)

"Pay? <u>Me</u> pay! Why, hell

All I want it for is to set up

A love-size portrait of a butterfly on"

54

From "the Teakettle Suggestion"
A man is led to good in small elevators
Soon villages and what amusing acrobats
When you depend on it
Harmony of wave's share & Old Shirttail
(My favorite cloud)
Now definitely one outranks none
On no account let them glue any generals on!
Not while you & I are in charge around here

The Little Bug Angel

He bangs his wings on the table!
Still no service!
What's the matter that waiter?
Wow! smell that roast beff!
Ah! he takes out a stick of dynamite—
Brr–uump! That should teach them!
But nothing happens!
Of course, obviously, the dynamite of an angel that size
Does not (fortunately) pack very much of a wallop.

IT'S ALWAYS TOO SOON OR TOO LATE

Fact is,

the train don't come on time for nobody

except those who should walk all the way to hell on their own backs

59

All things are
all things
True?
And if
not,
how not..
Then, my
little two-legged flea,
name me one
single thing
that is not

all
things!
Eh?

61

An Old Lady named Amber Sam

Piltched a REVERSE-STRIPE Zebra Off 2 Stalled Moving Van But since the Zee had no Built-In Spoon Any Soup she gave him lacked All Jiggable Tune So she put on an Old Pair of Baggy Pants And snuck Quietly out to a NEIGHBOR'S CAR AND shifted BOTH of its Headlights OntO the REAR-Bumper

COUNSEL FOR THE OFFENSE

Who gives his uncle a gear
For turning marbles into bears,
Shall always come when very near;
But who gives his aunt a stick
That will of bison make storks,
Must always loaf unless he works.
So if you wish really to thrive,
Act warmly toward that ball you throw—
For Summer's best jive is not snow;

64

65

Behind in his rent
Too tired even
to lie down
His best tin crown
badly dented

While his subjects
just loll around
munching rusty old
bottle tops

Certainly not
much

to pred   icate

A really driving
reign on

THE
KING
OF
LOG-
OOONA

66

Unless there are flowers
And years that begin in Spring
Unless the greatest sea
Is made of little waters
And life is least what it seems
Then I may not love thee

Which of us
is not
flesh?

Last

and first,
in that
common cause.
Beyond

this— I would like to be able
to say... to say more

68

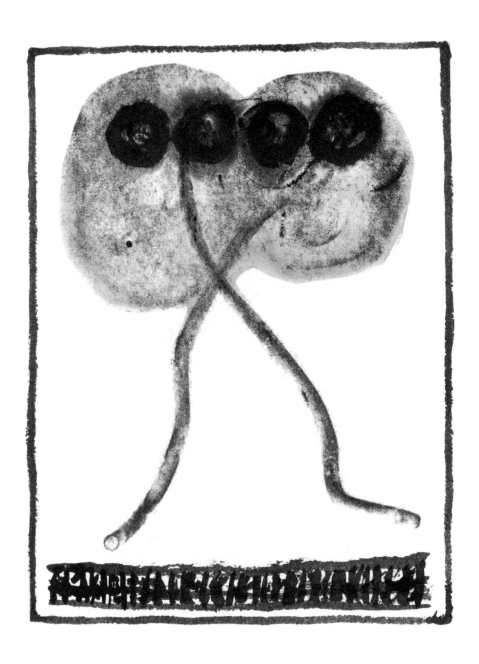

70

Who are you

Watching out of the water lily
Watching out of the oak tree
Daughter of the linnet's waking
Draughtsman of the tempest's oath
Who are you
Watching out of the wounded fawn
Watching out of the frolicking hare
O Designer of what awesome tidings

Sleeper Under The Tree

O shape the pillow
And shape the bell
Where no flower darkens
Where no thought weeps
Where no blade flashes
And no wave leaps
Where no hag is waiting
Where all beds are sweet
And where all our coats are unstained, my lord

The Question Is

What you doing there
On that dirty coalbarge,
You little puff-cheek rhino?
You can't be a prisoner,
You're sitting on the captain.
You can't even be very lonesome,
Not and play that kinda slidehorn!
Maybe it's you should be asking me
How come I'm over here, huh?

It's really lousy taste to live in a world like this.

Wait up here—
at the end of
the world.
For what—
tell me, what!

Same
thing
you're wait-
ing for now.

Point is,
you'll have
a better chance with
your wait when it's
all over

TIGER CONTEMPLATING A CAKE

Somebody had to be around here
Quite a while before he could

Build up to

figuring on a way

Why, with a

To excuse time spent

on this bauble

little more & trouble

He could be getting out a nice refreshing wildebeest-blood cola
Which didn't require no deposit for the bottle either

Why you running, pal?

You'll be all tuckered out by the time you get where you're goin'. Where I'm goin'? Do you reckon I'd be blurrin' ground like this if I had me any place to go.

Do you think that somebody will find us in time?

Yeah, I'm afraid so. That's the one thing they're bloody good at.

A

floating

Waiting at the bathhouse while a duck is

already having a fine swim for himself below

Sems different now they've taken the rose-colored penguins off this page

They'd slide up here laughing & having lots of fun like everything was going to turn out fine — against the law, I guess

82

Arrival

of

the

mailorder

dog

84

there's no
point saying
anything
except what
you
can't

Take your own hand and lead yourself
into the unneeding
place-of-you

Glory
never guesses

Ah! cherish the Smiling Moose
Who heaps basketsful of forgetmenots
Upon the blushing little beavers
And gaily dons gay-checkered knickers
To cycle off to cozify his Lovely Ella
With a rupple-dupple-dobbie-o
With a sneggle-keggle-owego
So you get with it too, dad
Love's worth all the sad

A SURPRISE FOR THE BAGPIPE PLAYER

Who expected no one would notice

That he'd gone home

Without even bothering to leave

None can leave where he's going

May all that have life be delivered from evil-willed suffering.

Hindu invocation

"Blessedness is not the reward of virtue, it is virtue itself"

Spinoza

"Everyman is me,

I am his brother. No man is my enemy. I am Everyman and he is in and of me.

This is my faith, my strength, my deepest hope, and my only belief."

Hallelujah Anyway

FOR MIRIAM

When this
is it,
eh!

With no more go-betweens
credentials
and
all that nose-counting
hokus-whosis forgotten as
we face up
to the real
business that has damn - well got
us all together here like we are

Kenneth Patchen

The concerns of the heart

Feeling, I must remind you, is the poet's sign — O let the print of her hurrying sandal be unrecorded in the meadow's thousand deaths yet upon his heart it has signed the angel's name. For him the distance of the world is never less than when he is forced to think how all he loves must soon be taken away

Kenneth Patchen

The World
Is Nothing
That Can
Be Known

in the shadow
we shall see
the color of
God's eyes
again

Patchen

beyond Love
there is no belief

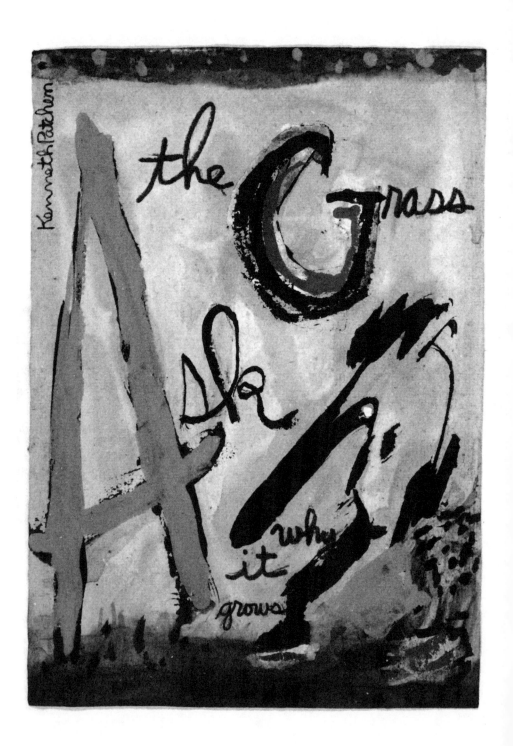

the Grass

Ask

why
it
grows

Kenneth Patchen

So when that nosey conductor comes round with that "Tickets please" dodge of his, we just plain up and hid the whole clackin' train—that's what we did

Patchen

103

ELE PHA NTS

and

ESK IM OS

are the sort of inventions makes me sure that God has a couple three-four kids of His own

Kenneth Patchen

The World's Not
Enough Really

For The
Kind of Rent
We Have To Pay
To Live In Us

Patchen

the day

cloaked in a

has followed me about

tatter of worn-out words

like some dog-like thing

Patchen

107

INSIDE THE FLOWER there is room for every sower whether he be stark monstrous-mad as all your "leaders" are or only some poor innocently crazy one who in his uncontrollable fear would deface & topple every last shrine and TOWER that are in any way at all still meaningful to mankind

110

THE
GROUND
KEEPER'S
D O G
AND THE
CASTLE
MASTER'S
CAT

Now they ran
round and round
Until what
They were sure
Was "This"
Often turned out
Never to be
Mostly
Not even "That"

111

LOVE (WHICH IN- CLUDES POETRY) IS TO SCIENCE AS THE FREE & BEAUTIFUL CATCHINGS OF A CHILD ARE TO THE VILE & UNRETURNING THROES OF THE HANGMAN

Kenneth Patchen

112

What the story tells itself
when there's nobody around
to hear it

Kenneth Patchen

TRIBUTE TO A GRANDFADDER FOOF

who is one of the little guys.

The impression of stairways,
Is not usually reckoned
More or less important
In terms of what may
Or may not have conspired
To cause one particular house (or dwelling)
To be erected in one place;
While, say, an identical structure (or coftwrage)
—But with a different roof (or chimneyance),
Peal-boned balustrades and
No door of any sort whatever —
So casually moved across town
In the mid-portion of the night,
With only two or three little policemen
In borrowed red paper vests
And spring-equipped girls' gym shoes
Bounding morosely alongleside it.

Kenneth Patchen

118

119

NOW IS THEN'S ONLY TOMORROW

As ever the trust of little birds
That the sky will be
Smart enough to appreciate
Their invention
Of flying

Kenneth Patchen

AH, YES! we'll please as we do

The birds are very careful of this world

Ha! a lot of good that'll do them!

(Behind those desks some mighty dangerous guys are sitting, Baby.)

Patchen

123

THE BURSO "DO-C-K-LE"

"It is," explained Mr Spugg, "a Horse-Not."
But so nice such; like him and you, I don't buy
Any // Crazy pigs! get into the streets
And tell them STOP IT!! got it all fixed
Blow everybody to hell you don't give a damn!
Run into the streets and yell God's shit down
On them! O blood of the butchered! O blood
That drips from every page of every school book,
From every whored-over pronouncement of brotherhood!
Children-killers in your lead-padded laboratories!
You Judas-paid pissers in the Face of Christ!
Skins of black, yellow, white-our brothers! I suppose
The butcher's price is the same - starvation, slavery - A-Bombs
Our brothers! this merchandice of death - I suppose
We should rejoice that the money-changers have

Been driven from our radioactive temples—& coins
Of flesh and blood made the standard of this trade,
Of our Golden Rule — 2 billions of souls already
Bartered away — Man has made hell! God is
Not dead. You have not even driven Him insane
With what — with the horror of what you plan to do!
But He weeps He weeps — O my brothers
He weeps // So I digress... O Mr Spuze, say
That the grass is green.. and that little dogs
Which go under wagons aren't always where —
I suppose that.... O but this, to be a Man—Not
The grass the sun the poor beautiful faces of men
My Bursо "Dockle" believes in you, he loves you
And so do I   Kenneth Patchen

Shaggy balls of fur, Enos! Who said those sesumatop-oppih were backward! Look at 'em bouncin' through that 'nilims pmaus! Y'know, there're more'n a couple sehctib-fosnos I'd like to see them a shakin' in the ugly mugs of!

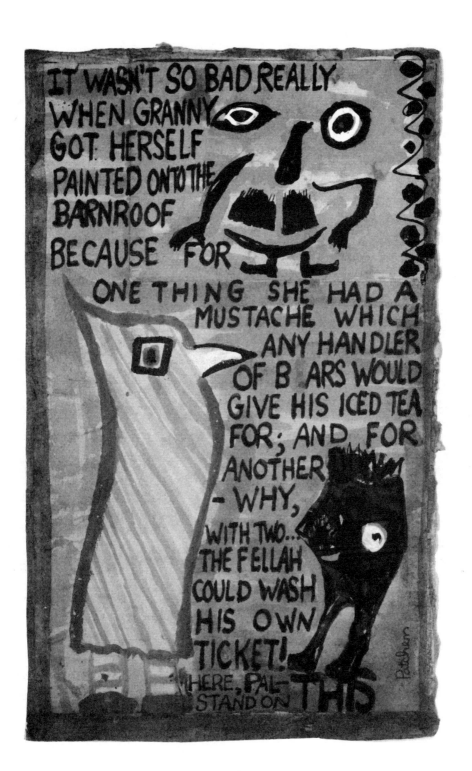

IT WASN'T SO BAD REALLY
WHEN GRANNY
GOT HERSELF
PAINTED ONTO THE
BARNROOF
BECAUSE "FOR
ONE THING SHE HAD A
MUSTACHE WHICH
ANY HANDLER
OF B ARS WOULD
GIVE HIS ICED TEA
FOR; AND FOR
ANOTHER
- WHY,
WITH TWO...
THE FELLAH
COULD WASH
HIS OWN
TICKET!
HERE, PAL—
STAND ON THIS

127

And Then Some
Fellows
Disguised
Lined Up
And Were

As Shelves
Along The Quay
Soon Bulging With
Food Stuffs, Hoe-
Handles Kero-
sene Lamps,
Crates Of
Geese, Doves,
Small Bears, Etc.

While This Was, Of Course, In Clear De-
fiance Of Ordinance 23-D, It Wasn't
Until The Following Tuesday That The
Culprits Were Discovered Having Them-
selves A Bang-up Good Time Down Behind
That Big Billboard Where The Road Turns

That Petey D Croos is a sly one!
What's he do but tell me he's go-
ing by boat so's
I'll figure him
maybe for a
bus or even borrowin'
his brother-in-
law's motorcycle,
see, and all the
time he's planned
on takin' a plane."
But I fooled him,
there he is whooping
it up in Omaha on my travelo's cheques,
while me, see— ha! I've had me a
hitch out to the Coast and back twice!

Kenneth Patchen

Now, When I Get Back Here, I Expect To Find All Of You Marching Through The Streets With Great Bunches Of Wild Flowers In Your Arms

Kenneth Patchen

132

The One

Who comes
To Quest-
ion
Him-
self

Has cared for mankind

Patchen

133

TREE-SLEEPING-
BEHIND-
LECTURER

O poor
thankless
vessel
Hast never
had thy feet
splashed
by a
Bear's
Tears
before

Kenneth Patchen

134

THE DAYDREAMS OF A KING differ from those of little spotty dogs by a ratio of maybe two-or-three hundred million to a rapidly shrinking none

Patchen

135

IN THE LONG RUN

This is a race where everybody ends up

in a tie, sorta

Kenneth Patchen

136

ead, pow! Tears of g
ck to just lay there a bi
uder tawny sounds that r
en   bodies oh it s
x   up - windo
                          erd yow m
                    wh   po
                    deno
           inu   itle Ch
est   en wh af bles
na   arrasa p   erq orl
ve   k wibb-e   een di
pt see him because it
oat reported on this s
erch and the whar   m
care oh stand forth while a
ed pink prowever when they rea
y since Joseph could not touc
ell appear beautiful on then w

139

141

PEACE PEACE PEACE PEACE

MERCY TRUTH FREEDOM

LOVE KINDNESS TRUST

PEACE OR PERISH

OR ALL MEN ARE DOOMED

FLOWERS BIRDS ANIMALS TREES

The issue
is no longer
war —
it is nothing
less than the
complete &
now almost
certainly
unavoidable
extinction
of every form
of life
on this planet

Kenneth Patchen

on our 28th Anniversary, June 28, 1962

for Miriam

142

THE WALKER STANDING

If you return
Before you go

Most fast-shuffles
Will seem pretty slow

Patchen

145

In the hippodrome they are always hoping that the next act will do it So there'll be no point in ever coming back or in going home Do you follow me?

Kenneth Patchen

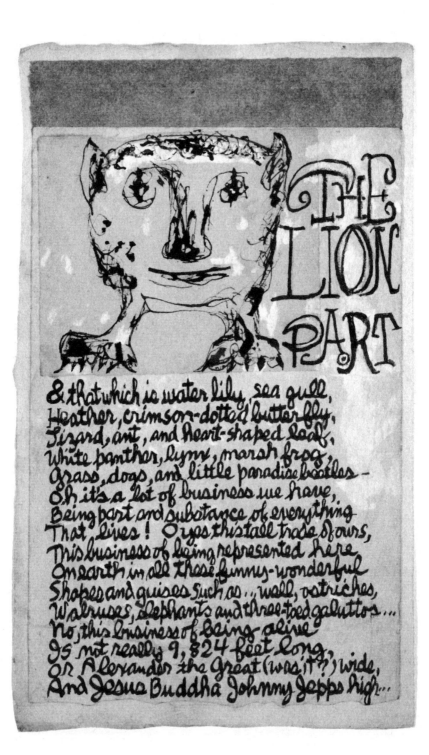

THE LION PART

& that which is water lily, sea gull,
Heather, crimson-dotted butterfly,
Lizard, ant, and heart-shaped leaf,
White panther, lynx, marsh frog
Grass, dogs, and little paradise beetles —
Oh it's a lot of business we have,
Being part and substance of everything
That lives! O yes this tall trade of ours,
This business of being represented here
On earth in all these funny-wonderful
Shapes and guises such as... well, ostriches,
Walruses, elephants and three-toed galuttos...
No, this business of being alive
Is not really 9,824 feet long,
Or Alexander the Great (was it?) wide,
And Jesus Buddha Johnny Jepps high...

148

The red flesh of the Rose and the blood of the Sea,
Engendered in one substance—The Glory of God!
Down it looks from the great stars in equal
Community on the vast universe of a gnat's wing,
Where, whirling together in that My starus
Of Oneness, which is all this world's sorrow,
This inseparable division, this estrangement in error
—For I see it makes there, over and over and over,
A statement of Life living away from us now!
Until the Sun's Wound is healed in our own hearts

Kenneth Patchen

BILLY BESTO & MR BUG

were over there easy and it runs up to them "Hello boys! how've you been." plenty nice hot soup couple beers

"Swell having you around! Keep up the good work, lads!" and then they all fell asleep

150

151

THE BEST HOPE

Is that one of these days the ground will get disgusted enough just to walk away~ leaving people with nothing more to stand **on** than what they have so bloody well stood for up to now

Patchen

152

The Walking-Away World

now no-
Got now-
what

body's
here
they never

Anyway

was

Kenneth Patchen

153

154

an interview with THE FLOATING MAN

But if you see no hope at all, isn't it sort of... well, a lie— all your talk about how human beings must love one another?

Yes, my friend, it is a lie. Already on the calendar blares the moment of all-freeing Truth... of Peace & Brotherhood of Equality & Integration —an end to misery and fear and hatred

Why, in that wonderful moment even their skins (had they skins) will be a quite acceptable color of cinder-black

Patchen

WHO'VE YOU BEEN TODAY

Know what they
used to say when

Song about all the while
things didn't go so hot?

Yeah that's when it
should be easiest to keep your cool alright

Kenneth Patchen

HAD GENERAL GRANT BEEN A XMAS TREE

You could take some little colored children—of which there aren't any other kinds—and explain to them that the reason he got drunk so much was because he knew they'd chop him down and smear him over with tin stars and fake snow and any other bloody rot they could dream up to make people believe it wasn't miracle enough just being a tree! That it was somehow more beautiful and wonderful (not to mention more profitable) to pretend you had something stuck there in the livingroom called "The Mystery Of The Christ Child." But, children (you'd warn them), at that rate, the next thing you know they'll be saying that you've had some kind of thing done you called "BEING CREATED EQUAL"! — And not only that…! "But regardless of your "race," "creed," and "color"!!" Look at them, children! Just look at them! Look at these insane, slavering excuses for men! Equal! Equal… they tell you! Not as a first step, mind you—but as a goal! as a heritage! as a glorious fulfillment—as a closing of ranks…

And the horror is,—that this time, this time… they're telling the truth.

— Kenneth Patchen

CHECK! QUESTIONS ARE THE BEST THINGS I ANSWER, BUB

Well, flip or hawl, if you'll pud 'em the repression, you got no call at all to go to the schoolmarm's, see; the last phone she had Old Chauncie Z. B. Varley beat to death with a hammer—said it reminded him of the clickity teeth of a tin bananer. But—right and ruddy! spoops, boods and—who do? Look, old buddy, it may be half past ten barn towels to you, but no ad jacent ever subtract me 'nuff t' shine down my leg! Go fry yersef some egg hair! Not with my tear-smeared ducks, yuh don't, boyo! weep up yer own damn come-long kingaling tooty trot, eh wot. Hist me up, O mither—unless you'd rither hire the lend of someone we'd both get a bang out of—like, say, any one of the Big Shots with the civilizing end of his Goddamned toadstool-spout-ing gun properly placed just where the temple-clearing bat of Christ would land were He anywhere alive just now. So.—I hope that tells you what you wanted to know, friend.

Yeah.... Thanks. But if that's your answer, I wonder what the hell it was I could have asked you

159

PRETTY SOON COMES
THE PUNCH LINE,
OLD MR. HE WHO—
OLD MR. HE HA-HA!
MADE THE LITTLE LAMB,
LITTLE LAMB-ALL SO
MEEK & SO VERY VERY MILD
LIKE IT WAS HIS OWN
LIL' CRADLE-ROCKIN' CHILD

† from a News Dispatch:

"For the third time a towering, fiery fist
— in the now all too familiar mushroom shape-
burst with a blinding roar above the desert
south of Algeria…

"Jubilant scientists reported that during
the so-called "hot" period immediately follow-
ing the blast, one of the control animals
in the concrete pits below gave birth!

"Of course the opportunities for truly reliable
investigations into what might be termed the
parabola or inverse declension-ratio of
mutations and such other…."

BETTER JOKE, THOUGH,
IF THAT DOPEY NUT WHO
COULDN'T SPELL BETTER
THAN Tyger HAD COME UP WITH Lam
— LIKE TAKE IT ON THEE

† Footnote For Posterity:
† THE ANIMAL - A BABY SHEEP
† THE TIME - A FEW DAYS
† BEFORE DEC. 25, 1960

Kenneth Patchen

162

164

You're faced wrong, that's what's the matter.

Not that the back of you looks much better. So pay me the fifty bucks you promised. I got me no great desire to continue longer in your hire, sire.

Patchen

Kenneth Patchen

Upon the book of the waters
The Autumn signature
of the Oak tree
it's written a springtime
pledge of you a consanguinity

166

167

A DREAM OF GOETHE DANCING WITH A FRIENDLY OSTRICH

169

Snow is the only one that leaves no tracks

Kenneth Patchen

171

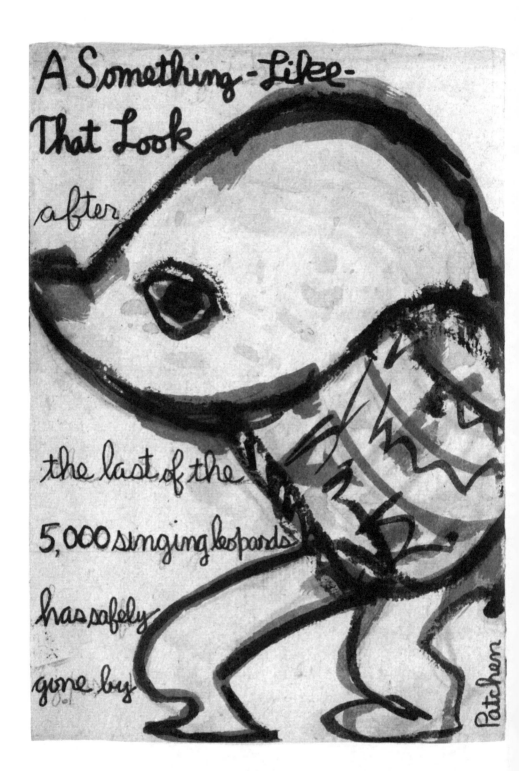

A Something-Like-
That Look

after

the last of the

5,000 singing leopards

has safely

gone by

Patchen

172

Whaleagle Rider

and th ere shal
l be s trange &
terrib le enc
ounte rs on t
h e way
to Our First Meeting
O My brother I
speak to none here

Kenneth Patchen

173

The Easy Hat-Eye Went To Sheperds Kim

Took her mother Tom
Along to short the moon
But I'd say it's no snap
Lookin' over the dam brim
At what they're doin' to Him
= To the Human Race, that is

Kenneth Patchen

174

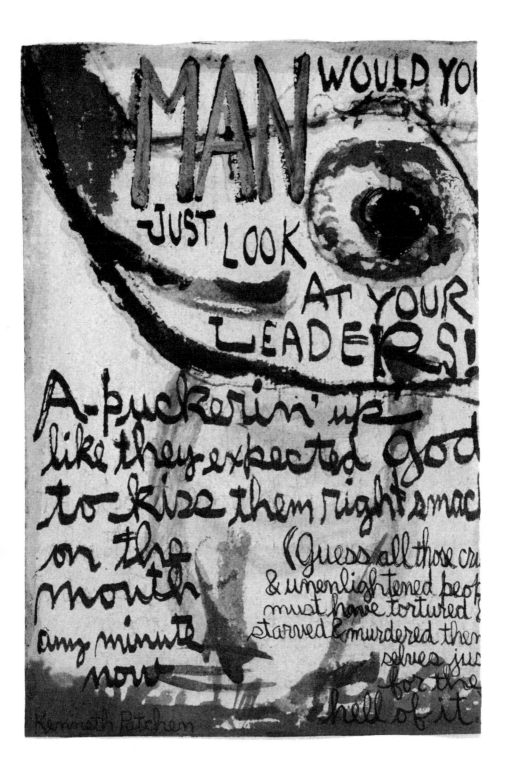

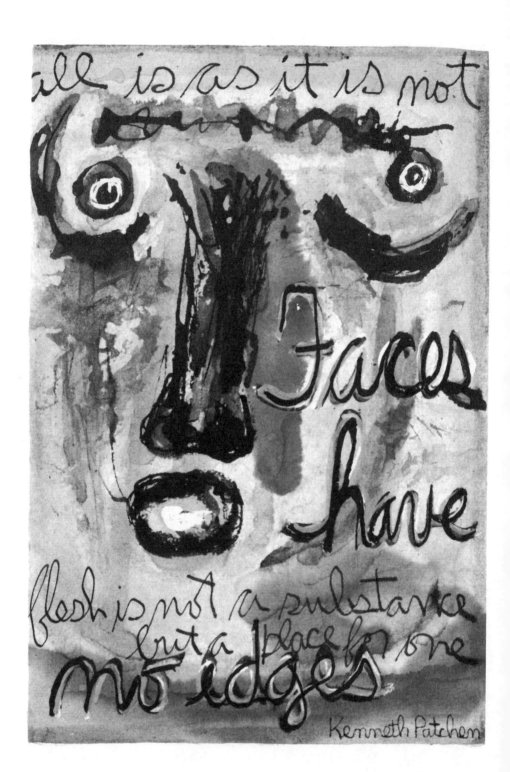

all is as it is not

Faces

have

flesh is not a substance
but a place for one

no edges

Kenneth Patchen

176

177

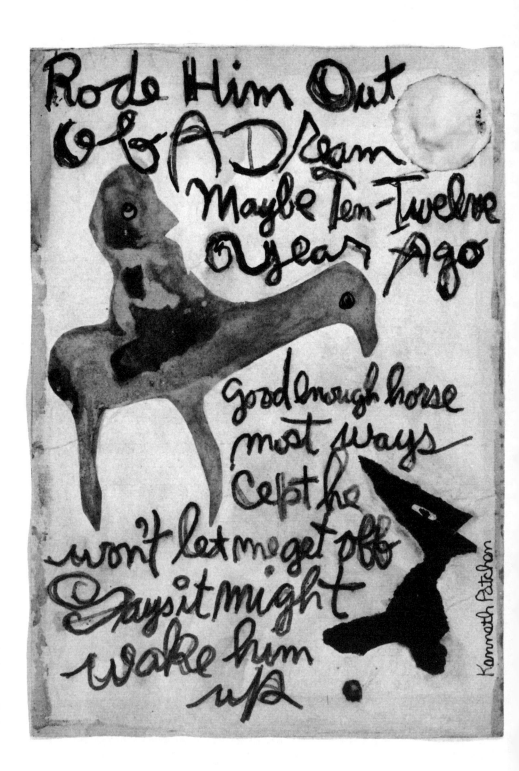

Rode Him Out
Of A Dream
Maybe Ten-Twelve
Year Ago

good enough horse
most ways—
Cept he
won't let me get off
Says it might
wake him
up

Kenneth Patchen

178

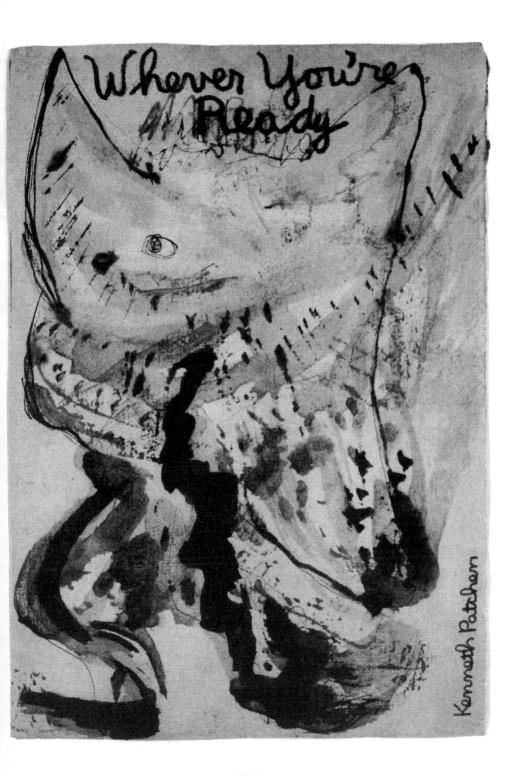

180

He's either going away or coming back And in between there you can put all the rest of it

Kenneth Patchen

A
feeling
of
passionate
mercy

the rest
doesn't
matter
a damn!

Patchen

But Even So

FOR MIRIAM

But Even So

They Don't Seem To Understand That Unless Someone Does Nothing Soon The Sky'll Sure Not Be All That's Up

Patchen

187

But Even So

go LOVING THEM — WITH ALL THEY ARE OR EVER WERE — YOU'LL OVERTHROW

Patchen

189

But Even So

This room, this battlefield

— Patchen

But Even So

But Even So

The Argument Of Innocence

can only be lost if it is won

195

But Even So

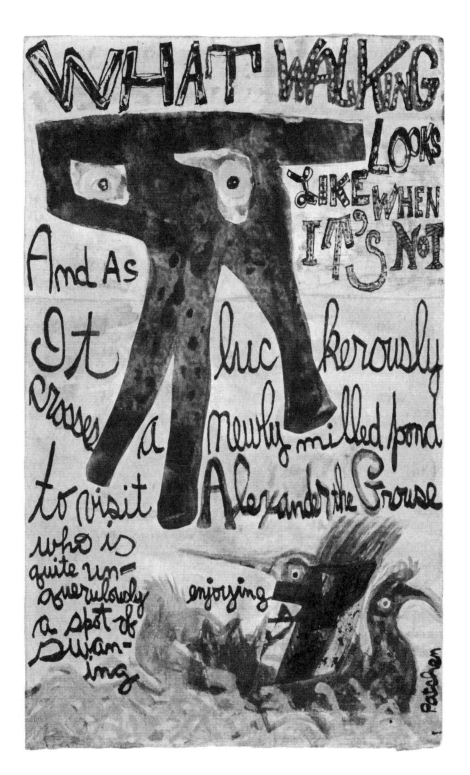

WHAT WALKING LOOKS LIKE WHEN IT'S NOT

And As It crosses a lucickerously newly milled pond to visit Alexander the Grouse who is quite un-gouruloudly enjoying a spot of swanning

Patchen

197

But Even So

The Hands of the Air

applaud the
Wonders of God
O Light & Life unending

199

But Even So

201

But Even So

QUIET

WE MUST NOT DISTURB

THE EVENING-BEING DEVICE

But Even So

CAN'T RECALL ME ONE REASON
FOR GIVIN' A DAM
WHERE "WHERE" WENT"

What a sweet buncha pigs
Bloody-footed hypocrites
Fouling up everything in sight
While you blather about saving
The world—with all the sincerity
And goodwill   of a snake

Shaking hands with a rabbit
But don't get me wrong.
As bastards go, you're long overdue
The hell is, you'll be taking the
Whole big beautiful world with you

205

But Even So

But Even So

209

But Even So

O tonight the stars is prayin' like melly they

jist had a raise in the rent *way yonder on Kyree Mountin

KAIN'T DENY THEY DID GIVE HIM A BANGUP HEADSTART

'Cause now Ole "Cougar Mash" Georgy Sue Jessup Jr an' still-king of New Kaintucky has got him a crown oiled with a couple-ten Smith & Wesson 44's and is reposedly in a permanently grave condition Pore Boy, pour!

but he didn't never get nowheres, My Daddy said, in that a-way

Patchen

211

But
Even
So

But Even So

215

But Even So

Caring is the only daring Oh you know it

Patchen

217

But Even So

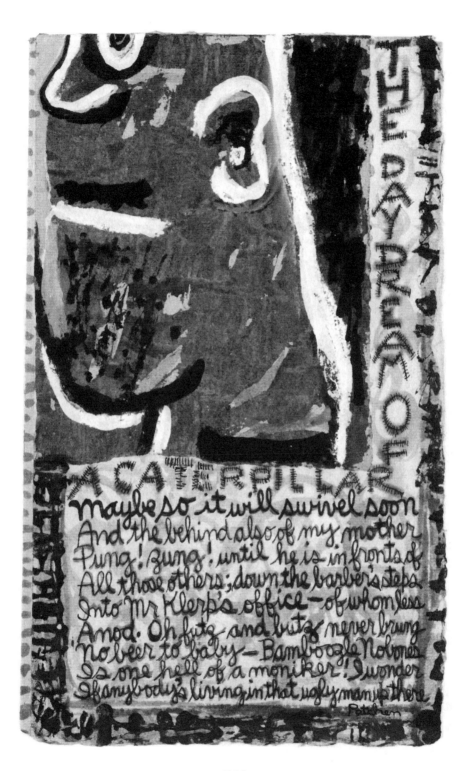

THE DAY DAVE DIE OU

A CATERPILLAR

maybe so it will swivel soon
And the behind also of my mother
Pung! Zung! until he is in fronts of
All those others; down the barber's steps
Into Mr Klerp's office — of whom less
Amod. Oh futz and butz never bring
No beer to baby — Bamboozle Nobones
Is one hell of a moniker! I wonder
If anybody's living in that ugly man up there

Peteson

219

But Even So

221

But Even So

223

But
Even
So

But Even So

At one time the grass was thought to be A people somewhat like the —Who were we? Q of that ardent regrom'cy, the silence pure of flesh to praise—unissuing epilogue to the unsaid—upon A blackened hill.. I was willing—for a garden, oh but Not to have the blood of the whole world dripping down upon it forever

Patchen

Alse whin darkes kom sae red Th'old Lass & Bread then rises frae Th'new Bride's pure Bed

But Even So

And Mr. Eggleg said "you wait there until I get back hear!" and he propped himself up near the telephone and hurries off, exactly one year later the phone rings - so he un props and says "Hello? Mr. Eggleg here." "I know who I am, you fool - what's the address? the buildings been torn down - hello! am I still there? (fact is, he is indeed: for Mr. Eggleg re propped comfortably and never was bothered by himself again.

But Even So

231

But Even So

Sure, Leroy,
There Is
A
Kindness
Of
Willing
& A Cruelty
Of Won'ting
Still—no dog ever
Doubt his dogness
The maple tree
Never mistake
Himself for
Any other cuss
But a man—
Who is us?

Patchen

233

The Christ
Who is
here
now

with
an Eye
staring out of the Sun
each of His Hands Sparrow
O the Rooster Rose
He is the Trout Tree the Hare Hound!
Light! Light! light

235

But Even So

237

But
Even
So

Mr Plickpoon of Darby & the Doon-adair Fly-swatter's Swallow's Daughter's Yodeling-Wooden-leg. Well! iffin now, say, the desire's on you to open a window, why this here's one method guaranteed positively to give the quickest and most complete satisfaction every single time out

Patchen

239

But Even So

241

But
Even
So

But Even So

245

But Even So

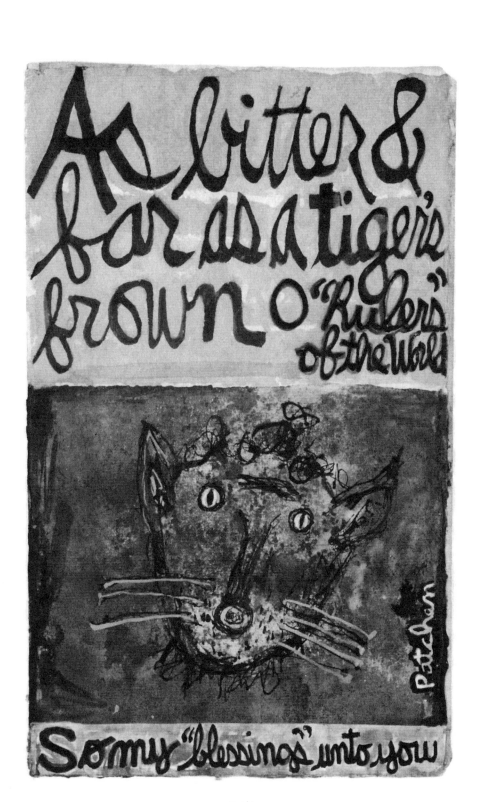

247

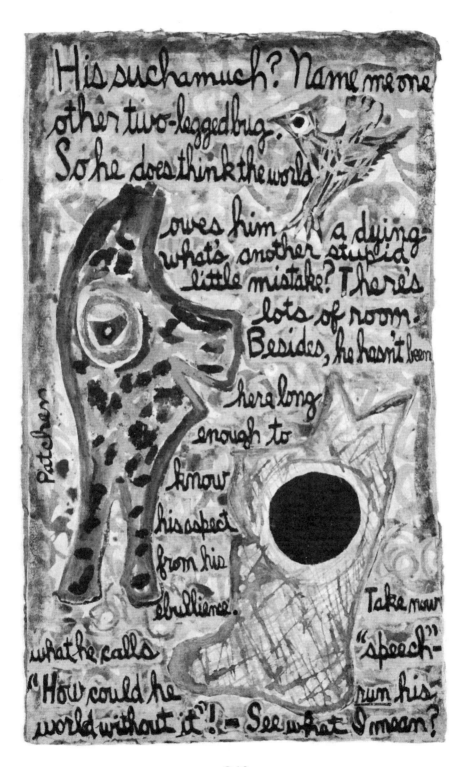

His suchamuch? Name me one other two-legged bug. So he does think the world owes him a dying— what's another stupid little mistake? There's lots of room. Besides, he hasn't been here long enough to know his aspect from his ebullience. Take your "speech"— what he calls "How could he run his world without it"! — See what I mean?

Patchen

But
Even
So

A Mountain's Knees Seldom Sneeze Unless he's allergic to the whis-dust of some of the more ferocious pine trees

Patchen

251

But
Even
So

O Fountain
Me A
Burning
Bell
O For None
Waken To
The Sight
& Cold
Falls This
Eternity of light

253

But Even So

THE Little Night-Eater Knows

Patchen

that "Sam's hand" (the Sioux word for bus wheel)

Will roll a many gasetious & rubblated Riders through the yi! yi! Zoom!

of far more buffalo-ed Kans-asses than good old Chief Screw-utoo ever knew ⊙ I GOT ME THOSE BALD EAGLE-SCALP-ING BLUES

Oh, oh... "Bullet Eye" Brexton, The Tree-Locker, has been by again — third time today that oak's been shriveled down to the size of a lil bitty tobaccah-chawin paw-paw bush. Wonder what Oedipus would've made of this?

Patchen

It's outside The Thing That Dances not in "our minds" Dreams "come in" The Fun of Christ Wholeness & Freedom! The universe is like a gigantic bird hopping up & down in such joy that from time to time it just topples over

Patchen

261

But Even So

The Crimson Leopard WALKS Through the SUN-SET TOWN

"Euripides I'll tear those, honey" —and Pozzo, drunk, goes on tugging away at the angel's sleeve

My Daddy was a carny clown

Patelson

265

But Even So

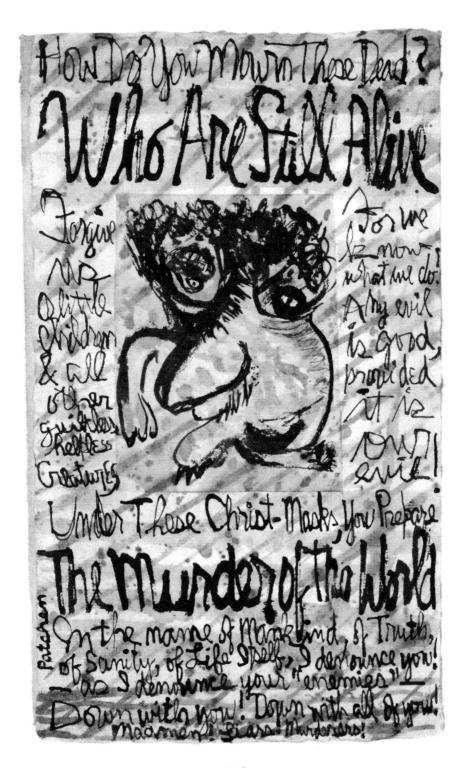

How Do You Mourn These Dead?
Who Are Still Alive

Forgive
Me
& little
children
& all
other
guiltless
helpless
Creatures

for we
k now
what we do!
Any evil
is good,
provided
it is
OUR
evil!

Under These Christ-Masks, You Prepare
The Murder of the World
In the name of Mankind, of Truth,
of Sanity, of Life Itself, I denounce you!
—as I denounce your "enemies"!
Down with you! Down with all of you!
Madmen! Liars- Murderers!

Patchen

But
Even
So

WE

Deserve Us

While the white lion sat smiling at
his merciless loom, see,
there's this
crownation
of kids
just sitting
down to their
lantern soup,
when this here
old grandma lady
up and squirts them
with her flame-
thrower

Patchen

269

But Even So

All That Leaves Is Here Always

Patchen

273

But Even So

ALSO AVAILABLE FROM NEW DIRECTIONS

PREFACE BY DEVENDRA BANHART

Now begins the revival of an eccentric virtuoso poet/visual artist whose work was admired by many of the 20th century's most unlikely "bobbysoxers": Charlie Parker, John Cage, Marlon Brando, Anaïs Nin, André Breton, Jasper Johns, Marianne Moore, Allen Ginsberg, Henry Miller, e.e. cummings, and many others. Like fabrics stitched into a crazy quilt, We Meet gathers five of Patchen's hard-to-find books (Because it is, A Letter to God, Poemscapes, Hurrah for Anything, and Aflame and Afun of Walking Faces) into a single volume introducing his work to a whole new generation of readers. It is chock-full of far-out poetry, rhythmic numinous prose, facetious fables, and jazzy drawings. Musician and visual artist Devendra Banhart complements We Meet with a celebratory, quixotic preface.

A New Directions Paperbook Original
NDP1115
$18.95 US/ $22.00 CAN
ISBN: 978-0-8112-1758-3